Stitched up

31 postcards from knitting-pattern hell

PRION

IN ASSOCIATION WITH THE ADVERTISING ARCHIVES

First published in 2001 by

Prion Books Limited

Imperial Works

Perren Street

London NW5 3ED

www.prionbooks.com

Compilation © Prion Books 2001

ISBN 1-85375-451-X

All images courtesy of The Advertising Archives, London

Many thanks to Suzanne and Emma

Printed and bound in China

by Leo Paper Products Ltd

Stitched Up

Moorland Double Knitting

Three sizes to fit 38-46 inch chest

Prion Books Ltd. Imperial Works, Perren Street, London NW5 3ED
for information email humour@prion.co.uk • image courtesy of the Advertising Archives

Prion Books Ltd. Imperial Works, Perren Street, London NW5 3ED
for information email humour@prion.co.uk • image courtesy of the Advertising Archives

Prion Books Ltd. Imperial Works, Perren Street, London NW5 3ED
for information email humour@prion.co.uk • image courtesy of the Advertising Archives

Prion Books Ltd. Imperial Works, Perren Street, London NW5 3ED
for information email humour@prion.co.uk • image courtesy of the Advertising Archives

Prion Books Ltd. Imperial Works, Perren Street, London NW5 3ED
for information email humour@prion.co.uk • image courtesy of the Advertising Archives

Stitched Up

SUPER NEW HATS
Frigate Holly Mohair

Prion Books Ltd. Imperial Works, Perren Street, London NW5 3ED
for information email humour@prion.co.uk • image courtesy of the Advertising Archives

Prion Books Ltd. Imperial Works, Perren Street, London NW5 3ED
for information email humour@prion.co.uk • image courtesy of the Advertising Archives

Stitched Up

To Fit 34-36 inch in bust

Beehive Fingering
or
Purple Heather
Fingering

Prion Books Ltd. Imperial Works, Perren Street, London NW5 3ED
for information email humour@prion.co.uk • image courtesy of the Advertising Archives

Prion Books Ltd. Imperial Works, Perren Street, London NW5 3ED
for information email humour@prion.co.uk • image courtesy of the Advertising Archives

Prion Books Ltd. Imperial Works, Perren Street, London NW5 3ED
for information email humour@prion.co.uk • image courtesy of the Advertising Archives

Stitched Up

Prion Books Ltd. Imperial Works, Perren Street, London NW5 3ED
for information email humour@prion.co.uk • image courtesy of the Advertising Archives

Stitched Up
FUN·FUR·KNIT

2 CUSHIONS
LADY'S BERET
MAN'S HAT

ONE SHILLING AND SIXPENCE

Prion Books Ltd. Imperial Works, Perren Street, London NW5 3ED
for information email humour@prion.co.uk • image courtesy of the Advertising Archives

Prion Books Ltd. Imperial Works, Perren Street, London NW5 3ED
for information email humour@prion.co.uk • image courtesy of the Advertising Archives

Stitched Up

Prion Books Ltd. Imperial Works, Perren Street, London NW5 3ED
for information email humour@prion.co.uk • image courtesy of the Advertising Archives

Stitched Up

STITCHED UP – POSTCARDS FROM KNITTING-PATTERN HELL

Prion Books Ltd. Imperial Works, Perren Street, London NW5 3ED
for information email humour@prion.co.uk • image courtesy of the Advertising Archives

DOUBLE CREPE WOOL

26 to 29 balls

Prion Books Ltd. Imperial Works, Perren Street, London NW5 3ED
for information email humour@prion.co.uk • image courtesy of the Advertising Archives

Prion Books Ltd. Imperial Works, Perren Street, London NW5 3ED
for information email humour@prion.co.uk • image courtesy of the Advertising Archives

Ladylike shawl and cardigan

To fit 32-38 inch chest

Prion Books Ltd. Imperial Works, Perren Street, London NW5 3ED
for information email humour@prion.co.uk • image courtesy of the Advertising Archives

Prion Books Ltd. Imperial Works, Perren Street, London NW5 3ED
for information email humour@prion.co.uk • image courtesy of the Advertising Archives

THE CLASSIC CLUBMAN

38 to 44 inch chest

Prion Books Ltd. Imperial Works, Perren Street, London NW5 3ED
for information email humour@prion.co.uk • image courtesy of the Advertising Archives

Stitched Up

101 Courtelle Crepe

knitted ponchos

Prion Books Ltd. Imperial Works, Perren Street, London NW5 3ED
for information email humour@prion.co.uk • image courtesy of the Advertising Archives

DIABOLO
for all the family

26 to 44 inch chest

Prion Books Ltd. Imperial Works, Perren Street, London NW5 3ED
for information email humour@prion.co.uk • image courtesy of the Advertising Archives

Prion Books Ltd. Imperial Works, Perren Street, London NW5 3ED
for information email humour@prion.co.uk • image courtesy of the Advertising Archives

Prion Books Ltd. Imperial Works, Perren Street, London NW5 3ED
for information email humour@prion.co.uk • image courtesy of the Advertising Archives

Prion Books Ltd. Imperial Works, Perren Street, London NW5 3ED
for information email humour@prion.co.uk • image courtesy of the Advertising Archives

Prion Books Ltd. Imperial Works, Perren Street, London NW5 3ED
for information email humour@prion.co.uk • image courtesy of the Advertising Archives

Golden Corniche
or Hi-Fi Chunky

32-40 inch

Prion Books Ltd. Imperial Works, Perren Street, London NW5 3ED
for information email humour@prion.co.uk • image courtesy of the Advertising Archives

Stitched Up

Double Knitting

32-39 in.
(81-99cm)

Prion Books Ltd. Imperial Works, Perren Street, London NW5 3ED
for information email humour@prion.co.uk • image courtesy of the Advertising Archives

Stitched Up

Prion Books Ltd. Imperial Works, Perren Street, London NW5 3ED
for information email humour@prion.co.uk • image courtesy of the Advertising Archives

Prion Books Ltd. Imperial Works, Perren Street, London NW5 3ED
for information email humour@prion.co.uk • image courtesy of the Advertising Archives